# Managing Up

## 20 MINUTE MANAGER SERIES

Get up to speed fast on essential business skills. Whether you're looking for a crash course or a brief refresher, you'll find just what you need in HBR's 20-Minute Manager series—foundational reading for ambitious professionals and aspiring executives. Each book is a concise, practical primer, so you'll have time to brush up on a variety of key management topics.

Advice you can quickly read and apply, from the most trusted source in business.

Titles include:

*Creating Business Plans*

*Delegating Work*

*Finance Basics*

*Getting Work Done*

*Giving Effective Feedback*

*Innovative Teams*

*Managing Projects*

*Managing Time*

*Managing Up*

*Performance Reviews*

*Presentations*

*Running Meetings*

**2◐ MINUTE MANAGER SERIES**

# Managing Up

Forge strong ties
Set clear expectations
Promote your ideas

HARVARD BUSINESS REVIEW PRESS

*Boston, Massachusetts*

Copyright 2014 Harvard Business School Publishing Corporation

All rights reserved
Printed in the United States of America
20

No part of this publication may be reproduced, stored in or intro-
duced into a retrieval system, or transmitted, in any form, or by any
means (electronic, mechanical, photocopying, recording, or other-
wise), without the prior permission of the publisher. Requests for
permission should be directed to permissions@hbsp.harvard.edu,
or mailed to Permissions, Harvard Business School Publishing,
60 Harvard Way, Boston, Massachusetts 02163.

The web addresses referenced in this book were live and correct at
the time of the book's publication but may be subject to change.

Library of Congress Cataloging-in-Publication Data

Managing up.
    pages cm. — (20-minute manager series)
  ISBN 978-1-62527-084-9 (alk. paper)
  1. Managing your boss.   2. Management.
  HF5548.83.M362 2014
  650.1'3—dc23
                        2013039033

# Preview

Nurturing a productive, mutually beneficial relationship with your manager starts with *you*, the direct report. That may seem daunting, but the art of "managing up" is one you can learn. This book walks you through the basics:

- Understanding your manager's priorities and pressures.

- Communicating your own needs and goals clearly and diplomatically.

- Building on common ground.

- Setting a positive tone for the relationship.

- Managing your boss's expectations—and your own.

- Navigating negotiations and disagreements.

- Strengthening your connection over time.

- Assessing the relationship and making adjustments.

# Contents

# Contents

# Managing Up

# What Is
# Managing Up?

# What Is Managing Up?

When you ask a friend how her job is going, she says, "Once I started managing up, things got a lot better." You cringe, thinking "managing up" smacks of political maneuvering, cozying up to the boss, or even outright manipulation.

Fortunately, when it's done right, managing up isn't any of those things. It can be a delicate business, no doubt. But it needn't involve power plays on the one hand or kowtowing on the other. Managing up is simply a conscious approach to working with your supervisor toward goals you both care about. The aim is to achieve a mutually beneficial relationship. This book gives you tips on how to do that.

## What managing up involves

Even though you're not the person in charge, you'll need to set a positive, productive tone for your relationship with your boss. And that requires certain skills:

- Knowing yourself and your manager well

- Managing expectations on both sides

- Listening with a keen ear

- Communicating in a clear, authentic voice

- Negotiating with diplomacy

- Monitoring the relationship as it progresses

- Making necessary refinements

You may be thinking, "Why not sit back and let my boss handle all this? Isn't the *manager* supposed to be the one who *manages*?"

But standing high and mighty on that principle doesn't help anyone. Besides, you'll miss out on the benefits of managing up, which you'll read about next.

## Why managing up is useful

Managing up helps you obtain the resources and buy-in you need to do your best work for your boss and your company. You, your manager, and your organization are interdependent: Only by recognizing that fact can you cultivate a strong, trusting relationship that allows you to get things done. You and your manager will then feel secure as you work together to solve problems rather than just talking about them, ignoring them, or sweeping them under the rug. And you will both feel more satisfied at work. Consider this example:

*Sam, a new director with a formal work style, replaced someone who had a looser, more intuitive approach. Carla, one of his direct reports, knew the importance of managing up. When she asked Sam how he preferred to receive information and updates, he said he liked reviewing reports before discussing them because it kept meetings structured and brief. So before her meetings with Sam, she sent him background data and discussion agendas. The result: highly productive meetings and innovative problem solving that improved the entire team's performance. Sam's transition was smooth, and he and Carla quickly developed a friendly, efficient working relationship.*

Contrast Carla's experience with that of Larry, another of Sam's direct reports:

*Larry found Sam's style too controlling. He was not especially interested in managing up or learning what Sam valued, so he didn't ask for direction. He seldom provided background information before meetings and often felt blindsided by Sam's questions when they sat down to talk. Consequently,*

*Sam's meetings with Larry lasted longer—and accomplished less—than those with Carla. Sam found them frustrating, and he attributed delays on projects to Larry's inefficiency. So Sam gave Larry negative performance reviews and didn't put him forward for promotions.*

Carla's efforts at managing up clearly benefited everyone involved: Sam, her team, and herself. But failing to manage up means more than simply missing out on benefits. It can be a risky proposition, as Larry's case illustrates. Refusing to learn about and accommodate your manager's preferences can lead to misunderstandings about your skills and your dedication to your work.

"Tuning in" to your manager, however, is only part of what it takes to avoid problems like Larry's and reap rewards like Carla's. You must also know yourself and navigate the differences between the two of you—that's what we'll cover next.

# Knowing Your Manager—and Yourself

# Knowing Your Manager— and Yourself

Managing up is a constant process. It takes keen observation and a willingness to adjust your behavior on a daily basis. But once you and your boss have built a trusting relationship on a solid foundation, cultivating it becomes easier and less time-intensive. The first step in getting to that happy place is identifying where you and your boss stand, both professionally and personally.

# Roles

Beyond your obligations to each other, you and your manager have specific roles to play and people to whom you're accountable. In short, you each have a web of complex relationships to maintain and responsibilities to fulfill. Acknowledging those realities can help you see the world from your boss's point of view.

It's also essential to understand your manager's priorities and pressures—and to map them against your own. Locate points of overlap and those of potential conflict, perhaps by marking them on an organizational chart. The visual evidence can expose hidden risks and opportunities in collaborating with your manager.

For example, look for chances to support your boss in work she's doing for her own manager. Ask how you can help—and suggest ideas of your own. Suppose, for instance, she could use an extra set of hands on an exciting project with a tight deadline. Propose taking on certain tasks that complement your skills and interests. You'll get to participate in higher-level work, your boss will get more done, and throughout the project you'll be showing—not just telling—her that your goals and hers go hand-in-hand.

Of course, differences in power can make some subordinates, especially those who are themselves managers, react in unhealthy ways. Management experts John Gabarro and John Kotter highlight two problematic responses to a boss's authority:

- *Counterdependency:* when you unconsciously resent your boss, perhaps even see her as an institutional enemy. Counterdependent subordinates may start arguments (especially with authoritarian bosses) just for the sake of fighting.

- *Dependency:* when you swallow objections—or anger—and comply even when your boss makes a poor decision. Dependent subordinates stew rather than express honest opinions.

If you recognize a bit of yourself in either of these profiles, consider how your natural reaction to authority in general may be damaging your relationship with your boss. Then think about ways to respond more constructively, as in the previous example, where offering to help your boss leads to a more efficient division of labor and the chance to contribute to a desirable project.

## Strengths and weaknesses

Once you know your manager's strengths, you can find ways of working together that bring out the best in both of you. You can also appreciate how she's using those strengths to support team and company goals—and tactfully promote those accomplishments to others in the organization. Bosses appreciate, and often reciprocate, that kind of advocacy.

Though you may have a pretty clear idea of what makes you a good employee, pinpointing your manager's strengths can be tougher to do. You'll certainly want to observe her as she pursues objectives and interacts with others. You can also get valuable insights by talking with coworkers who know your boss better than you do, especially if you've just started reporting to her.

Having done that bit of informal research, list your manager's strengths alongside your own and note the similarities and differences. Points of overlap—say, you're both analytical and data driven—can spark camaraderie and strengthen your relationship. Differences needn't be seen as problems—they can signal opportunities to complement your manager.

You may, at times, bemoan your boss's shortcomings or even feel thwarted by them. But that's a prescription for frustration. Instead, think of recognizing her weaknesses as an important step toward achieving your common goals. Figure out where your manager needs assistance, and step up to offer it.

For example, if your manager has a tough time meeting deadlines, identify the obstacles that typically stand in the way. Offer to tackle those tasks for her if they're in your purview—or to perform a supporting role if they're not. Even a friendly reminder a week or so ahead of a deadline can go a long way. A collegial, in-person nudge is more likely to prompt action than a sterile ping on an electronic calendar.

Zero in on your own weaknesses, as well. To develop an effective partnership, you need to know when to lean on your manager, not just when she can lean on you. If your weaknesses and hers overlap in some areas, those may be points of "friendly commiseration" on an emotional level. On a practical level, they may reveal where the two of you need outside support.

## Work styles

As Carla did in our earlier example, ask your manager how she likes—and does not like—to operate. It's important to know her general preferences ("Stop by my office rather than sending me e-mail") and to scope out specifics ("Updates on this project should come to me every Thursday by noon").

Your boss may not think to articulate her overall style or her day-to-day approach to getting things done, assuming they're obvious. But chances are, she also won't mind answering a few thoughtful questions about how she likes to work. Table 1 lists some questions you might try and related actions you can take. The fact that you're asking demonstrates your interest in efficiency, your capacity for foresight, and your attentiveness as a direct report.

As presumptuous as it may seem, it's also important to clarify your own work style with your manager in the interest of practicality and transparency. But don't forget the power difference discussed earlier: Show a willingness to modify your own approach to arrive at a mutually suitable style of interaction with your boss. In leading by example, you may find that

TABLE 1

## Work style questions and actions

| Questions to ask | Sample actions to take |
| --- | --- |
| Do you prefer formal or informal delivery of information? | • If your manager favors formal delivery—reports, spreadsheets, and so on—prepare agendas for your meetings with her and give her relevant documents in advance. Also send frequent, regular updates on your assigned projects.<br><br>• If she likes informal sharing, avoid burdening her with documents before you chat. Update her on projects only at crucial junctures or when you need specific guidance. |
| How do you like to process information? | • If she wants to study it by herself before discussing, supply it in written form.<br><br>• If she prefers to react and ask questions on the spot, present the information in person. |
| How would you describe your management style? | • If she likes to have a hand in day-to-day operations and decision making, touch base with her often.<br><br>• If she prefers to delegate, keep her abreast of essential developments, but handle most of the details on your own. |
| How do you address problems and conflicts? | • If she prefers open debate, be prepared for lively, spontaneous exchanges, bearing in mind that her goal is to air ideas, not to express anger or disapproval.<br><br>• If she favors a more reflective approach, show that you have analyzed the situation by stating your observations plainly. Give her the chance to do the same before you both decide on a course of action. |

*Source*: Adapted from Liz Simpson, "Why Managing Up Matters," *Harvard Management Update*, August 2002, 4.

your manager extends the accommodation in the other direction, adjusting her practices a bit to suit what matters most to you.

## Motivators

At every employee's core, from entry-level worker to CEO, are the things that drive her to do good work. Identifying what motivates your boss is a key component of managing up.

Sometimes it's easy. For example, if your manager is driven by a desire to trim costs, she has probably shared that publicly. You might support that aim by streamlining redundancies in processes or systems that you oversee.

But some motivators run deeper. Perhaps your manager is a "big picture" person, inspired by vision, and prefers to leave details to team members like you. In that case, don't dive into minutiae when you give her updates; briefly sum up what you've done and explicitly state how it supports her overall goals. By contrast, if your manager craves specifics, you might choose an illustrative example as a cross-section of your work. You'll engage her with the intricacy of what you're doing rather than boring her with the broad spectrum of your tasks.

Similarly, during check-ins with your manager, talk about what motivates you. That equips her to make engaging assignments and connect you with people in her network who will inspire you. Report back to your manager when you find a specific project exciting—make it easy for her to give you the kind of work that makes you tick.

# Managing Expectations

# Managing Expectations

S etting clear expectations is essential to building a productive relationship with anyone, and your boss is no exception. Though it's a two-way street, give your manager's priorities top consideration—after all, she's in charge. Identify what she wants from you and do your best to deliver it.

## Know what your manager expects

Your boss will want you to fulfill your key responsibilities, meet her standards for performance, and achieve objective measures of success. But you can't do any of that until you understand how she defines those responsibilities and standards and which metrics she'll use to gauge your progress.

Ask her to describe what she's looking for in your work. If she doesn't articulate her expectations clearly, try writing them up and sharing that informal document with her to make sure you've captured them accurately. Then schedule a follow-up conversation or ask for written feedback—whichever your manager prefers. You'll want to revisit those expectations periodically, in case they change.

Every job—and every manager-subordinate relationship—is different. But most managers expect some combination of these behaviors from their direct reports:

- *Offer ideas.* Make creative suggestions for innovation or improvement. If you have an idea, err on the side of sharing it rather than squelching it.

- *Manage your own direct reports competently.*
  Coordinate their efforts, foster camaraderie,
  write useful and specific performance reviews,
  support their professional development,
  step in when one of them falls behind, and
  manage crises with skill and patience. When
  your boss needs to hear bad news about one
  of your direct reports, deliver that news
  yourself.

- *Collaborate with peers.* Work collegially with
  others toward your manager's goals. Overcome
  differences with coworkers, even if you dis-
  like one another, with the aim of getting the
  job done.

- *Lead initiatives.* Raise your hand for cross-
  functional projects, particularly those that
  involve implementing new ideas. Make clear
  how your involvement is consistent with your
  manager's expectations of you.

- *Stay current.* Keep abreast of industry trends, marketplace developments, advances in technology, and other events outside the company that may affect its success. Bring your insights to bear on your work.

- *Drive your own growth.* Seek out professional development opportunities. This can mean taking classes or pursuing a degree—but it doesn't have to. You might simply expose yourself to new ideas and people or accept challenging assignments that enhance the value you add to your team and your company.

- *Be a player for all seasons.* Stay positive even during hard times. That will inspire and motivate your direct reports, your peers, and your manager.

Managers differ in how much value they place on each of these behaviors. Tailor your emphasis according to your boss's expectations and work style.

## Set your own expectations

To meet your manager's expectations, you must set your own sights ambitiously yet realistically. That means identifying and sharing your—and your direct reports'—needs for direction and resources, as well as respecting your manager's limits in fulfilling your requests.

Discuss all this in a face-to-face meeting, and ask for feedback. By being explicit, you'll clarify your mission, stake out the boundaries of what's feasible, and show your manager that you are deliberate in your approach. If your expectations don't match your manager's, try to negotiate an agreement that works for both of you. (See "Negotiating with Your Manager" later in this book.)

You must also set realistic expectations for those who can help you meet your boss's goals: your direct reports, managers in other departments, customers, suppliers, independent contractors, and others inside or outside the organization.

When collaborating with others in your sphere of influence, ask yourself these questions:

- How do they perceive my manager and the work I'm doing for her?

- Which of my manager's goals can they help me meet?

- What's the most effective way to communicate those goals to them?

- How can I best persuade them to help?

- What problems can I help *them* solve in return?

You won't have formal authority over most people around you, just as you don't have authority over your manager. So you can use some of the same techniques to manage *out* that you've used to manage *up*: offering ideas and solutions, providing feedback, and sharing reactions and perspectives.

Meeting your boss's goals and expectations may require you to relinquish control and empower others.

That may involve delegating tasks—even those that come with significant responsibility—to direct reports. It may also mean coming up with creative ways to share responsibilities with superiors, subordinates, and peers.

In managing up, you're doing that kind of deft interpersonal coordination all the time—and constantly getting better at it. But, as you'll see next, there are limits in how far that skill will take you.

## Understand the limits of managing up

No matter how clearly you and your manager set mutual expectations, you won't be able to control every outcome. And when you can't find common ground, more often than not, you will be the one who has to give. The better you get at managing up, the more often you'll agree with your boss and the less vexing compromises will seem when you don't. As the relationship gets stronger, the need for effort diminishes, but it doesn't disappear. Nor does the power difference between you.

Keep these basic limitations in mind:

- I can influence my manager, but ultimately I am not in charge.

- My own goals are important, but my boss's take precedence.

- My manager sets more expectations for me than I do for her.

- I have more to prove to my boss than she has to prove to me.

Reading that list may make you sigh, but two things should comfort you. First, the list is short, so the possibilities far exceed the limits. Second, you can greatly expand the possibilities by skillfully managing up.

# Communicating with Your Manager

# Communicating with Your Manager

E ffective communication takes a deft touch when you're managing up. If your attempts to persuade are too obvious, they may not succeed. Yet you need to be deliberate in your approach. This chapter helps you walk that fine line.

## How to listen and observe

As you engage with your boss in everyday activities, try to identify the messages behind her speech and behavior. The words and deeds matter, of course, but the values that underlie them often mean more. Listening with a keen ear and observing with a sharp eye can make all the difference in understanding, not just labeling, your manager's communication style.

Consider the statement "My door is always open," which many bosses make to their direct reports. That seemingly transparent sentence can have a variety of meanings. Here are three examples:

Rebecca:

*When she says, "My door is always open," Rebecca means it literally. To foster honesty and camaraderie, she wants people to feel free to approach her in person at any time. It invigorates her when a direct report has an idea and spontaneously pops into her office to share it. When a problem arises, she wants to hear about it immediately, because it reassures her that everyone is working as a team. She bristles when people who come in to speak to her close the door behind them. Indeed, she worries that colleagues will see a shut door as evidence of hypocrisy. If Rebecca must talk with someone in complete privacy, she reserves a meeting room.*

Raul:

*Raul's open-door policy is one that he expects people to observe in spirit, not in absolute terms. The door to his office is open 90% of the time, but when a deadline is imminent, he shuts it so he can concentrate, especially if he is writing. He wants people to see him as easy to approach and "always available," but he views e-mail and team meetings as legitimate ways for people to reach him. If someone considered him a hypocrite for shutting his door once in a while, Raul would think that the person lacked common sense.*

Janice:

*Janice works in a cubicle with low walls, as do all of her direct reports, so she doesn't even have a door. To her, an "open door" is merely a metaphor for how colleagues work together. She doesn't want people to fear making mistakes, even in front of her. But she also places a high premium on giving folks the mental space to do their work quietly and to consider proposals deliberately before acting on them. She wants her direct reports to share novel ideas but expects them to submit those in writing before asking other people to react. To Janice, an open door does not mean an "instant response," a phrase that she often uses when describing slipshod work.*

As varied as these "open door" interpretations are, at least Rebecca, Raul, and Janice give their employees something to go on. Some managers don't even have an explicit policy about how—and how often—to communicate with them.

Whatever your manager's preferred style of interaction, you'll probably need to do a little investigating to figure it out. Start by asking yourself these questions:

- *Is my manager a listener or a reader?* Listeners want to hear information first and read about it later. Readers prefer to see a written report before discussing it with you.

- *Does she prefer detailed facts and figures or just an overview?* If she thrives on details, focus primarily on accuracy and completeness; if she prefers an overview, emphasize the clarity and crispness of the main idea.

- *How often does she want to receive information?* Your manager may always want to receive updates at specified junctures or she may have different thresholds for each project, such as daily reporting on critical endeavors and periodic updates on secondary initiatives.

Every exchange of information with your manager has implications for productivity. These tips will help you be more efficient:

- When discussing deadlines, use specific language. Pinpoint a certain date—even a specific hour, if appropriate. Avoid vague commitments like "sometime next week," "ASAP," or "as soon as we can get to it."

- Be honest about what you can and cannot handle. When you commit to an assignment, clearly identify what resources you need to get the job done.

- Explicitly identify your objectives each time you communicate with your manager.

- Ask questions to clarify what you don't understand. Inquire about opportunities for follow-up in case you think of other questions later.

## How to present problems and opportunities

One of your manager's main jobs is responding to news, both bad and good. She must factor brand-new problems and opportunities into existing goals, plans, and work flows. You can help by following this process:

1. *Describe the impact in clear terms.*  In discussing a problem, pinpoint how it affects your work and your organization's performance. In presenting an opportunity, outline the potential benefits. Explain exactly how solving this problem or seizing this opportunity will help you and your manager achieve your shared goals.

2. *Identify your solution or approach.*  Recommend a specific plan, but also present other options. Outline the pros and cons of each possibility and explain why you favor the one you do.

3. *Flesh out the implications.*  Do your best to identify everyone who has a stake in the matter. Give concrete examples of the risks and benefits for each stakeholder. If you have tested your solution or approach on a small scale, present the results and what you have learned from them.

4. *Fine-tune your plan.* Actively engage your manager in developing a final action plan to increase the likelihood of smooth implementation. Doing this will demonstrate your commitment to ensuring success.

# How to disagree with your manager

When you communicate with your manager, you're looking for common ground. If you don't find it, however, it's important not to panic or retreat. You may think that disagreeing with her will make her perceive you negatively or trigger a defensive reaction. But managers want to make better-informed decisions, so they often seek other perspectives. Indeed, most of them report that they don't hear enough alternative points of view.

To disagree constructively with your manager, show respect and understanding for her point of view, and demonstrate that you care about achieving the best result for the organization. Here are some ways to do that:

- *Link your idea directly with your manager's and your organization's goals.* This will show that you are motivated by a desire to collaborate and achieve shared aims, not to be contrary.

- *Provide suggestions that your manager can act on, not just objections.* You can say something like, "How about contacting others in the industry who have used this system to see if they're having the same problems? Would you like me to draw up a list of people to call and schedule some time with them?"

- *Explain how your idea can prevent pitfalls.* Identify those pitfalls in precise terms, and present supporting data to show that your proposal is fact-based rather than emotional.

- *Offer a range of options.* Binary choices ("Your
  way or my way") are likely to meet resistance.
  Suggesting a few possibilities signals your flex-
  ibility and invites your manager to respond in
  kind.

- *Give verbal and nonverbal feedback.* Use
  phrases such as "I see" or "I know what you
  mean." Nod or smile to indicate understanding.

- *Avoid "hot button" language.* If, for example,
  your boss always recoils when someone describes an approach as a "best practice" or "the
  next big thing," find another way to express
  yourself.

- *Reflect your manager's concerns as you speak.*
  For instance, "I understand that you're worried
  about how this new plan will work, and I was
  initially concerned about that, too. But when
  I did some research, I realized something
  important . . ."

Moments of disagreement are usually a bit uneasy, but a trusting relationship with a boss allows room for them. Indeed, navigating differences of opinion successfully and with maturity can make the relationship even stronger. And having a solid bond with your manager makes negotiating with her easier.

## DEALING WITH A TOXIC BOSS

David is a high-performing project manager with a talent for creating dashboards. He likes his work but is frustrated by his repressive, micromanaging boss, Thaddeus. Thaddeus drones on about the high point of his own (now stalled) career, calls unnecessary last-minute meetings, and frequently tries to one-up his direct reports. Meanwhile, David has managed to impress Irving, an executive VP in the company's

*(continued)*

## DEALING WITH A TOXIC BOSS

European division, enough to receive a job offer, but it's a lateral move with no increase in pay.

What should David do? Experts in managing up recommend three options:

1. *Stay Put.* Consultant and author Gini Graham Scott thinks that David should try to remain where he is for now. Taking the job that Irving offers would be the equivalent of announcing, "This is the level where I'm supposed to be." Plus, Thaddeus might see a lateral move within the organization as a personal slight, and the bad blood could trail David to his new position. To cope, David can form a supportive network of colleagues, explore interests outside work, and even attempt—subtly and nonconfronta- tionally—to get his boss to change some of his crazy-making behavior. For instance, David

might describe (in a memo or face-to-face meeting) what he thinks his boss wants from him and offer ideas on how to achieve it. That would place the focus on David's work, not on his boss's actions. If he can't tolerate working for Thaddeus any longer after trying to improve the dynamic, he should look for an opportunity outside the company.

2. *Make the lateral move.* Brad Gilbreath, an associate professor of management at Colorado State University-Pueblo and a former HR manager, says David should escape from Thaddeus and accept the job with Irving. Research shows that bad bosses' behavior can lead to high blood pressure, depression, and other health problems in their subordinates. Working for

*(continued)*

## DEALING WITH A TOXIC BOSS

Thaddeus is clearly taking a toll on David's psychological well-being—and probably on his physical health as well.

3. *Create a new option.* Lauren Sontag, an executive coach and former head of development at JPMorgan Chase, says David should set clear and explicit boundaries with Thaddeus. David might dread the thought of discussing what's bothering him, but having that difficult conversation could dramatically improve Thaddeus's behavior. That said, staying with Thaddeus (whose career is stalled) might be more of a dead end than accepting Irving's lateral offer— because if your boss isn't moving up, you probably aren't either. So David should consider a third option: carving out a new role for himself that capitalizes on his expertise in creating

useful dashboards. He might even propose
setting up a dashboard "center of excellence"
to serve both Thaddeus and Irving, and adding
a junior employee who would report to him.
That way, he could meet both their needs *and*
advance in his career.

*Source*: Adapted from David Silverman, Gini Graham, Brad Gilbreath,
and Lauren Sontag, "Surviving the Boss from Hell," *Harvard Business
Review* (September 2009).

# Negotiating with Your Manager

# Negotiating with Your Manager

Negotiating with your boss is an art. You're persuading someone in authority to see things from your perspective—and then to take action. Your negotiations may focus on tasks such as overseeing projects, securing resources, winning assignments, or getting buy-in or approval for new ideas. Or they may concern issues of personal satisfaction such as work/life balance or flexible scheduling. Either way, you'll need to:

- Establish your credibility

- Identify priorities

- Communicate strategically

# Establish your credibility

Negotiation is most effective when the other party respects your judgment. If you can, lay the groundwork before negotiations begin so your reputation precedes you. But whether or not you have that opportunity, it's wise to gently but confidently establish your credibility by emphasizing your trustworthiness and expertise.

Here are some tips for earning your manager's trust in a negotiation:

- *Be sincere.* Express your conviction that your proposal is worth your boss's time and attention, and explicitly state your commitment to it. You might say, "I really believe in this, and here's why . . ."

- *Highlight your track record.* Remind your boss of commitments you've previously honored— and of the positive results that ensued.

- *Welcome suggestions.* Listen to your manager's concerns and consider how you might account for them in your proposed plan.

- *Put your boss's interests first.* When your manager knows that you care about her goals and needs, she'll be more likely to trust your ideas.

- *Be candid.* Own up to your proposal's limitations. By showing that you're aware of them, you'll demonstrate that you're realistic and thinking about how to avoid problems.

To establish your expertise:

- *Present your research.* Gather as much information as you can about the idea you're proposing, but summarize it succinctly. Back it up with your most compelling data. Lay out counterarguments to show that you've considered potential objections.

- *Gain firsthand experience.* Participate in pilot projects to deepen your knowledge; join cross-functional teams to broaden it. Share what you've learned with your boss, either in writing or during check-ins.

- *Cite trusted sources.*  Name the people you've spoken with about your ideas, recount their reactions and experiences, and refer your manager to them when that's feasible. Testimonials from folks your boss respects will go a long way.

- *Offer proof of concept.*  Initiate your own tests, particularly if you're not able to gain firsthand experience in an existing forum. For example, you might run a mini-experiment with your own direct reports before suggesting that your manager try it with you and others who report to her.

With trust and expertise in your arsenal, you're more likely to succeed in any negotiation you undertake.

# Identify priorities

Topics for negotiation with a manager cover a wide field, but a common one is how to prioritize your assignments: what tasks to accomplish, in what order, and when.

You should certainly manage your time as independently as you can (you may irritate your boss if you require a lot of oversight). But when you deviate from established routine—as problems arise, for example, or as you take on new responsibilities—you may have to renegotiate due dates, time allotments, and related details with your boss. Never wait until you're about to miss a deadline to reprioritize your tasks with your supervisor. Demonstrate foresight, and preempt problems by proposing alternatives, as discussed earlier.

In negotiating with your manager about work priorities:

- *Show that you are aware of all the projects for which you're responsible.* Even if part of your proposal is to delegate a particular task to someone else, don't speak about that task dismissively.

- *Specify clearly what you can and cannot do in the time you have.* Propose more than one option for reconfiguring what's on your plate. And be open to alternatives that your manager suggests.

- *Ask for help setting deadlines for new work to avoid slowing down other projects.* Put together simple charts that show where competing schedules overlap; they can be fabulous visual aids as you plot out the new trajectories.

- *Follow up with an e-mail to seal the deal.* Putting the results of your negotiation in writing gives you and your manager a handy reference point as you implement changes.

Your manager understands the importance of priorities. After all, as a manager, she must reassess them all the time. Showing her that you, too, can think ahead will facilitate your negotiations because she'll see that you know where she's coming from.

## Communicate strategically

In negotiations, persuasion is paramount. So the way you package your message is as important as the message itself. A few pointers can help:

- *Avoid "you"-centered language.* Use words like "I," "we," and "both" so you won't sound accusatory. For example, say "I'm not clear about this point" rather than "You didn't make that clear." Or "Can we can meet that schedule?" rather than "Do you think your schedule is feasible?"

- *Take a win-win approach.* Indicate how your ideas will benefit your manager and the organization, not just you. Zero in on performance. For instance, say "Delegating these reports will free me up to spend more time pitching to clients."

- *Collaborate.* Don't just "dump" a problem on your manager and ask her what to do about it. Offer to set up a meeting so you can think through it together: Pick her brain, and share ideas of your own.

When negotiating with your manager, don't think of it as arguing for something you want. Instead, view it as searching for a solution that works for both of you. The aim is not tit-for-tat compromise—it's mutual benefit.

# Monitoring the Relationship

# Monitoring the Relationship

No matter how well you and your manager work together, never take the relationship for granted. Like any significant connection between two people, it requires nurturing and periodic reflection. Assess the strengths and weaknesses of your relationship with your boss every few months by revisiting these 10 questions:

1. Have I taken the primary responsibility for managing my relationship with my boss?

2. Am I aware of my manager's expectations for me? Are they realistic?

3. Is my manager aware of what resources I need to meet those expectations?

4.  How much does my boss know about what I've been doing for the past few months? If she doesn't know enough, how can I correct that?

5.  Am I reliably meeting my commitments? If not, how can I rectify shortcomings?

6.  How well do my manager and I get along on a daily basis? Do we need to address any conflicts?

7.  Do our oral and written interactions occur with ease? If not, how can I make our communications more seamless?

8.  Do we trust each other? What can I do to increase the level of trust?

9.  Do I back up my boss when I talk to others about her and execute her goals?

10. What could I do to support my manager more effectively?

Obviously, ripples can surface in any relationship. When that happens, smooth them out as soon as you notice them. Periodic assessments using these 10 questions can reveal the not-so-obvious problems that fester when left neglected. You might even track progress by counting how many questions raise concerns each time you monitor the relationship. If the number increases over time, that may signal a systemic problem in the relationship. If the number decreases, your connection is probably getting stronger and more productive.

The point is simply to be vigilant without creating undue worry. Remaining attuned for signs of regression—and nipping them in the bud—will ultimately make progress more likely.

# Learn More

## Books

Harvard Business School Publishing. *HBR's 10 Must Reads on Communication.* Boston: Harvard Business Review Press (2013).

The best managers know how to communicate clearly and persuasively. How do you stack up? If you read nothing else on communicating effectively, read these 10 articles. We've combed through hundreds of articles in the *Harvard Business Review* archive and selected the most important ones to help you express your ideas with clarity and impact—no matter what the situation. Leading experts such as Deborah Tannen, Jay Conger, and Nick Morgan provide the insights and advice you need to: (1) pitch your ideas successfully, (2) connect with your audience, (3) establish credibility, (4) inspire others to carry out your vision, (5) adapt to stakeholders' decision-making styles, (6) frame goals around common interests, and (7) build consensus and win support.

Harvard Business School Publishing. *HBR Guide to Managing Up and Across*. Boston: Harvard Business Review Press (2013).

Are your working relationships working against you? To achieve your goals and get ahead, you need to rally people behind you and your ideas. But how do you do that when you lack formal authority? Or when you have a boss who gets in your way? Or when you're juggling others' needs at the expense of your own? By managing up, down, and across the organization. Your success depends on it, whether you're a young professional or an experienced leader. This book will help you: (1) advance your agenda—and your career—with smarter networking, (2) build relationships that bring targets and deadlines within reach, (3) persuade decision makers to champion your initiatives, (4) collaborate more effectively with colleagues, (5) deal with new, challenging, or incompetent bosses, and (6) navigate office politics.

Useem, Michael. *Leading Up: How to Lead Your Boss So You Both Win*. New York: Three Rivers Press, 2001.

When your supervisor is micromanaging you, lacks competence in a particular domain, or has no long-term vision, you're not powerless to improve the situation. You may be able to turn things around by "leading up" (another term for managing up). Useem draws on vivid examples to show how it's done—describing, for example, how a U.S. Marine Corps general reconciled his six bosses' conflicting priorities. Just as leading up yields many benefits, failing to do so can have dire consequences, as Mount Everest mountaineers discovered during a dangerous climb.

## Articles

Bossidy, Larry. "What Your Leader Expects of You." *Harvard Business Review*. April 2007 (product #R0704C).

The success of an executive team depends heavily on the relationships the boss has with his or her direct reports. Yet the leadership literature has had little to say about what is expected in those relationships—on either side. Larry Bossidy, formerly the chairman and CEO of Honeywell, shares what he calls "the CEO compact," detailing the behaviors a leader should look for in subordinates and what they should be able to expect in return. A CEO's best people, he says, know when a situation calls for them to get involved. They generate ideas, put the long-term good above short-term goals, develop leaders among their people, anticipate how world events may affect the company and its competition, expose themselves to new people and ideas, and accept demanding assignments to drive their own growth. On the other side of the compact, the boss should provide clear direction; give frequent, specific, and immediate feedback; be decisive and timely; demonstrate honesty and candor; and offer equitable compensation. Executives who aren't lucky enough to have such a boss can create a compact with their own subordinates, Bossidy says, and demonstrate by example. The result will be to improve team and company performance and accelerate individual growth.

Field, Anne. "Truth or Consequences: Dealing with a Conflict-Averse Boss." *Harvard Management Communication Letter.* April 2005 (product #C0504A).

When a boss can't communicate directly about problems, the performance of her employees suffers. People routinely receive less-than-forthcoming performance appraisals and thus get little clear guidance on developing their strengths or overcoming their weaknesses. They find it difficult to get the resources they need to complete a project because the boss refuses to stick up for them. And their productivity decreases because they have to spend an inordinate amount of time and effort finding out what the boss really thinks of them. Learn some strategies for forcing needed discussions without making your boss feel she's being backed into a corner.

Gabarro, John J., and John P. Kotter. "Managing Your Boss." *Harvard Business Review.* January 2005 (product #R0501J).

In this classic HBR article, first published in 1980, the authors explain that the manager-boss relationship is one of mutual dependence. Bosses need cooperation, reliability, and honesty from their direct reports. Managers, for their part, rely on bosses for making connections with the rest of the company, setting priorities, and obtaining critical resources. It only makes sense to work at making the relationship operate as smoothly as possible. Successfully managing your relationship with your boss requires that you have a good understanding of your supervisor and of yourself, particularly strengths, weaknesses, work styles, and needs. Once you are aware of what impedes or facilitates communication with your boss, you can take actions to improve your relationship. You can usually establish a way of working together that makes both of you more productive and effective.

Harvard Business School Publishing. "Five Questions About Interviewing Your Prospective Supervisor: With Rich Wellins." *Harvard Management Update*. October 2004 (product #U0401B).

Most hiring managers look at the personality fit between themselves and job candidates, but few prospective employees give it much thought, and many later discover that they and their supervisors are mismatched. Wellins describes how to initiate frank discussions with prospective supervisors—and how to get telltale glimpses into their personalities. This process is as relevant to considering a new internal assignment as it is to interviewing for a position at a different company.

Harvard Business School Publishing. "Narcissistic Leaders." *Harvard Management Communication Letter*. June 2000 (product #C0006E).

Many companies are discovering that "there is no substitute for narcissistic leaders in this age of innovation," as Michael Maccoby has pointed out in *Harvard Business Review*. Maccoby was referring to those brash and thoroughly egotistical visionaries who so often head up companies. Learning how to communicate with such bosses is nothing short of a strategic management skill. This article offers some pointers for dealing with the raging narcissist in the corner suite.

Kanter, Rosabeth Moss. "The Cure for Horrible Bosses." *Harvard Business Review*. October 2011 (product #F1110E).

In her HBR column, Kanter argues that the best way to counter the effects of a horrible boss is to cultivate a strong network of colleagues.

Sasser, W. Earl, Jeffrey Pfeffer, and Paul Falcone. "Challenge the Boss or Stand Down?" *Harvard Business Review*. May 2011 (product #R1105M).

In this fictional case study, Tom Green, an aggressive young sales executive, has been promoted to senior marketing specialist by his division VP. The VP has warned him that he'll have to learn fast and work well with his new boss, Frank Davis. On the job, Tom finds himself at odds with Frank and challenges him openly at a well-attended meeting. Frank begins to formally document deficiencies in Tom's performance, and the division VP falls in line with Frank. With his back against the wall, Tom must carefully consider his next move. Harvard Business School professor W. Earl Sasser presents the case; Jeffrey Pfeffer, of Stanford University, and Paul Falcone, of Time Warner Cable, offer their expert commentary.

## Podcast on HBR.org

Meister, Jeanne. "Manage Up and Across with Your Mentor." January 31, 2013.

Jeanne Meister, coauthor of *The 2020 Workplace: How Innovative Companies Attract, Develop, and Keep Tomorrow's Employees Today* and a partner at Future Workplace, which helps organizations redefine their corporate learning and talent management strategies, discusses how your mentor can help you manage up and across. From sharing deeper institutional knowledge with you to tips for understanding what's happening at your boss's level to figuring out which battles to fight and how to fight them, this podcast offers a host of ways your mentor can help you work more effectively across your organization.

# Sources

## Primary sources for this book

Harvard Business School Publishing. Harvard Manage-
   Mentor. Boston: Harvard Business Publishing, 2002.
Harvard Business School Publishing. *Pocket Mentor: Manag-
   ing Up*. Boston: Harvard Business School Press, 2008.

## Other sources consulted

Silverman, David, Gini Graham Scott, Brad Gilbreath, and
   Lauren Sontag. "Surviving the Boss from Hell." *Harvard
   Business Review*, September 2009 (product #R0909B).
Simpson, Liz. "Why Managing Up Matters." *Harvard Man-
   agement Update*, August 2002 (product #U0208A).

# Index

# Notes

# Notes

# Notes

# Notes

# Notes

# Notes

# Advice you can quickly read and apply.

Looking for more? Get up to speed fast on the most essential business skills with HBR's 20-Minute Manager Boxed Set. Whether you need a crash course or a brief refresher, this 10-volume collection of concise, practical primers will help you brush up on key management topics.

## HBR's 20-Minute Manager Series

**Available in paperback or ebook format.**

- Creating Business Plans
- Delegating Work
- Difficult Conversations
- Finance Basics
- Getting Work Done
- Giving Effective Feedback
- Innovative Teams
- Leading Virtual Teams
- Managing Projects
- Managing Time
- Managing Up
- Performance Reviews
- Presentations
- Running Meetings
- Running Virtual Meetings
- Virtual Collaboration

**HBR.ORG/20MINUTES**

**Buy for your team, clients, or event.**
Visit hbr.org/bulksales for quantity discount rates.

Harvard
Business
Review
Press

# Smart advice and inspiration from a source you trust.

If you enjoyed this book and want more comprehensive guidance on essential professional skills, turn to the HBR Guides Boxed Set. Packed with the practical advice you need to succeed, this seven-volume collection provides smart answers to your most pressing work challenges.

## Harvard Business Review Guides

Available in paperback or ebook format. Plus, find downloadable tools and templates to help you get started.

- Better Business Writing
- Building Your Business Case
- Buying a Small Business
- Coaching Employees
- Delivering Effective Feedback
- Finance Basics for Managers
- Getting the Mentoring You Need
- Getting the Right Work Done

- Leading Teams
- Making Every Meeting Matter
- Managing Stress at Work
- Managing Up and Across
- Negotiating
- Office Politics
- Persuasive Presentations
- Project Management